My Nan Speaks Nanish

Jane Williams

My Nan Speaks Nanish
(and other poems for kids and wannabes)

Illustrated by Lisa Morgan

Acknowledgements

Some of the poems in this collection first appeared in
australianchildren'spoetry.com.au
Children's-Stories.net
Our Home is Dirt by Sea (Walker Books, 2017)

My Nan Speaks Nanish (and other poems for kids and wannabes)
978 1 76041 594 5
Copyright © text Jane Williams 2018
Copyright © illustrations Lisa Morgan

First published 2018 by
Ginninderra Press
PO Box 3461 Port Adelaide 5015
www.ginninderrapress.com.au

Contents

No such thing	7
My Nan speaks Nanish	8
Mystery man	10
Clementine's in quarantine	12
The adventurous aunties	15
If I were a kid	16
Three Lunar Limericks	19
The heebeegeebees	21
I could tell you a story	23
When I grow up I'm going to eat white bread	25
Whatshisname	27
Turtle Time	29
Ducking down for the night	31
Children of the fairy queen	33
Surprise party	35
Pearl	37
Ship in a bottle	39
Sir BB	41
Some Kids	43
Have you seen my lizard	44
Home	46
Gotta love that dream	49
The seagull ~~squawks~~ speaks	51
Animal dreams	53
Awoooooooooooooo	55

No such thing

No such thing as monsters
I'm absolutely sure
So is Mrs Werewolf
Who rents the house next door

No such thing as monsters
A scientific fact
I've seen it writ in blood
Sincerely signed Count Drac

No such thing as monsters
My sources can't be wrong
I heard it from a friend
Of a friend of King Kong

No such thing as monsters
The neighbours all agree
Dr Jekyll, Mr Hyde,
The Frankensteins and me

No such thing as monsters
And really I should know
Mummy unwrapped herself
Just now to tell me so

My Nan speaks Nanish

My Nan speaks Nanish, not Hippo or Hag.
It's a tricky language I'd really like to snag.
It's a scrumptious secret wild horses couldn't drag
but Nan won't let the cat out of the bag!
My Nan speaks Nanish not Gothic or Goop.
Running in circles, jumping through hoops
she calls me chicken noodly soup.
Possum. Pumpkin. Favourite fruit loop.
My Nan speaks Nanish, not Thai or Turkey.
Spying on the neighbours what does she see?
Pishposh! Codswallop! Fiddle-de-dee!
Wagging tongues barking up the wrong tree.
My Nan speaks Nanish, not Belgium or Bear.
She'd teach me if she had time to spare
but it's half past a freckle, a quarter past a hair,
the proof's in the pudding and hen's teeth are rare.
My Nan speaks Nanish, not Egg or Eggplant.
When old photos lull her into a trance
she's caught and led in a merry old dance
by teasing bees knees and fancy ants pants.
My Nan speaks Nanish not Frisian or Finch.
A lick and a promise will do in a pinch.
Though life, she admits, is never a cinch
on matters of manners she won't budge an inch.

My Nan speaks Nanish, not Creole or Coot.
Warts make her worry and beans make her toot.
When she married my Pop it was a hoot,
they dressed in glad rags and a monkey suit.
My Nan speaks Nanish, not Persian or Pie.
It's a tricky language, I don't know why
but when wishes are fishes, pigs will fly
my Nan will speak Nanish, and so will I!

Mystery man

I met a man I didn't know
But he knew me from go to woe

Your name I think is Paris Post
He said deadpan as eggs on toast

You enjoy pine and mountain breeze
A little wine and too much cheese

Your tan is airbrush number one
The colour of your hair is plum

Who are you I asked by and by
Soothsayer? Psychic? Private eye?

No said the man, nothing so odd
Though mine is an interesting job

I move at dawn from house to house
Not quite as quiet as a mouse

And at each one I find a clue
To him and her and you and you

Strong and quick and light on my feet
I store the secrets of the streets

I am my own apologist…
Your neighbourhood garbologist!

Clementine's in quarantine

Clementine's in quarantine
and can't come out to play,
she spent a week in outer space
and just got back today.

Running rings round Saturn,
eating moony cheese
catching Martian Red Eye
and a nasty Neptune wheeze.

She can't see past the sunspots
and the stardust in her eyes,
there's a buzzing in her ears
that could be Venusian flies.

The freckles on her face
are glowing in the dark,
I touched one oh so lightly
and felt a little spark!

Her fingers and her toes
are all accounted for,
she didn't lose a single one…
in fact she gained some more…

It's just this look she gets
when asking what's for tea
when she licks her furry lips
and looks longingly at me!

So Clementine's in quarantine
and can't come out to play,
she spent a week in outer space –
I wish that's where she'd stayed!

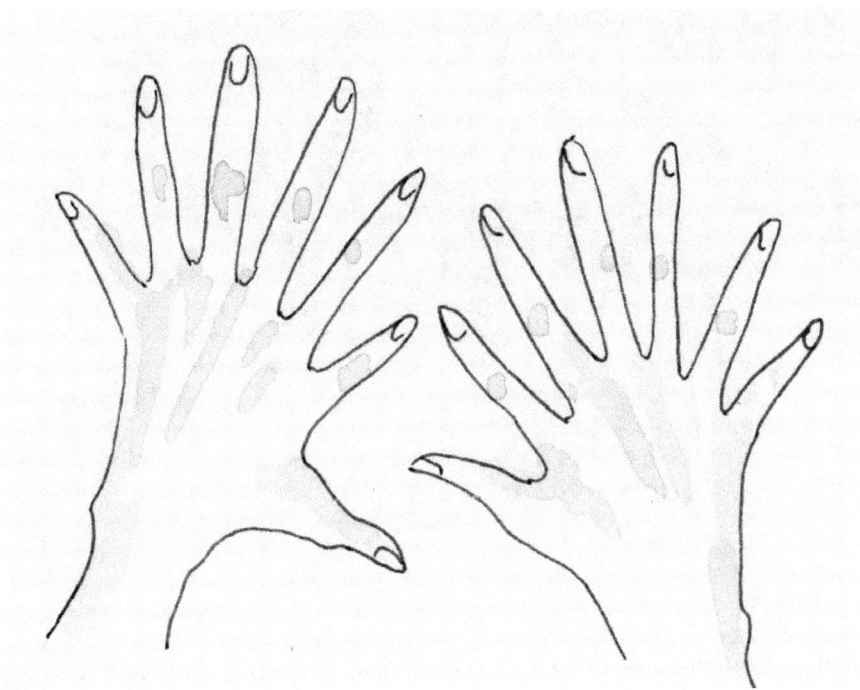

The adventurous aunties

Aunty Finola festooned a fella
And brought him over for tea
He wasn't refined but I didn't mind
So they sat him next to me

Aunty Chicory challenged a chappy
To a game of air guitar
The neighbours winced but I didn't flinch
She'll make a smashing rock star

Aunty Bethany borrowed a buddy
For a wrestling match in Greece
They wrestled in jest and I was impressed
(That she gave him back in one piece)

Aunty Marlene misplaced a young man
When the circus came to town
It wasn't her fault. I saw him bolt
When the lion swallowed the clown

If I were a kid

If I were a kid
instead of a child
I'd call Mum, Nanny
and I'd be wild !

A wild non-child
never keeping still
I'd nibble her handbag
then run for the hills.

If I were a kid
and not just a child
I'd call Dad, Billy
and I'd be wild !

A wild non-child
always butting in
I'd kick up a fuss,
and wear a silly grin

But I am what I am,
and that's all I can be
except on those days
when it's plain to see…

The child in the kid.
The kid in the child.
Each a little bit tame,
and a little bit wild !

Three Lunar Limericks

*

There once was a monster from mars
Who ate so many mars bars
He pulled with a thread
Every tooth in his head
And stuck in some neighbouring stars

*

Griselda Goon was sent to the moon
(her nose played a terrible tune)
She travelled at night
At the speed of light
In a perfectly soundproof balloon

*

I once met an alien who thought
We humans a very strange sort
Why is it he said
Shaking one of his heads
That none of you pickle your warts?

The heebeegeebees

Granddad's got the heebeegeebees
He says they're pestering things
They like to catch him unawares
They like to get under his skin

Do they live in houses like us I ask
No said Granddad they don't

Do they live in trees like birds I ask
No said Granddad they won't

Do they live in caves like bears I ask
No said Granddad they wouldn't

Do they live in rivers like crocodiles
No said Granddad they shouldn't

Do they I ask live under my bed
And Granddad grinned
Well…maybe…he said

I could tell you a story

I could tell you a role-swapping story,
one sure to make you think twice.
Filled with shy and retiring dragons
and some fire breathing mice.

I could tell you a caper of daring,
a thrilling trailblazing tale,
one to lift you from life as you know it
and fly you beyond the pale.

I could tell you a legend of mystery,
a slowly unwinding yarn,
one to keep you supposing and guessing
till the last page works its charm.

I could tell you a science fiction,
imported from outer space,
with creatures from stars and planets.
And one who's wearing your face.

I could…but it's late and you're sleepy,
your mouth a yawn, it would seem.
And your eyes (so big!) must be heavy,
so goodnight my love…and sweet dreams…

When I grow up I'm going to eat white bread

and a whole packet of chocolate biscuits
on my own. Just to be clear, the biscuits
will be chocolate and I will be eating them
on my own that is by myself, I mean
without sharing.

Because I'll be a grown-up
and when it comes to sharing,
grown-ups get to decide What, When, Who.
So I'll be deciding –
chocolate biscuits. Any time. Me.

First I'll tear the corner of the packet, just the corner,
and closing my eyes take one long sniff. Aaaaahhhhh
that's the stuff, that chocolatey biscuity smell. Next
I'll oh so slooooowly, oh sooooo carefully pull back
the wrapping then run the tip just the tip of my tongue

across the top of each biscuit, each chocolate biscuit
in that whole packet of chocolate biscuits –
the one I'm going to eat after the white bread
on my own by myself without sharing
when I grow up.

Whatshisname

Pop tells Nan
Old Whatshisname rang
And he has to go see about a wee
Dog or horse
Give us a kiss he says
For luck
But Nan tucks her lips away
Far as she's able
That's no way she says
To put bread on the table

Still Pop goes on out
And when he comes back in
I ask him Poppy whatdidja bring?
And that's when I learn
The dog was a lemon
The horse a crying shame
And that Pop will never forget
Old Whatshisname

Turtle Time

I'm taking my turtle time.
I've no wish to cram or collide.
For a turtle would never hurtle,
hurry, harangue or hound.
It's just not done and in no way fun
for a turtle to bolt or bound.

I'm taking my turtle time.
No need to squabble or whine.
Free to nibble all day
as the plants float my way.
No desire to twitter or purr,
to bother with feathers or fur.

I'm taking my turtle time.
I don't envy the tiger or lion,
I could never keep up the pace,
(no instinct to pounce or make haste).
How exhausting, risky and crude
to always be chasing one's food!

I'm taking my turtle time
and I must say it's quite sublime!

Ducking down for the night

Ducking down for the night
one eye open one closed,
I've still got you in sight
as I wind down and doze.

A clever duck that's me,
a deft, dabbling drake –
when my body's half-asleep,
my brain is half-awake.

Children of the fairy queen

The children of the fairy queen
are seldom heard and seldom seen

in landscaped parks or city zoos,
highway lanes or shopping queues.

But if you wander off the map
and dare to cross the fairy gap

you'll see them dancing through the night –
a canopy of silver light

illuminating steps so rare;
a free spun whirlwind in the air,

a tapping of the earthen core,
a shuffling of the ocean floor,

and always one with fiery eyes
to show you dreams of other lives.

Surprise party

I'm putting on a party
For fancy and for fun
A hush hush celebration
A shindig just for one

Oh everything is planned
From the presents to the punch
From clowns to fireworks
And flowers by the bunch

I made the cake blindfolded
I did not lick the bowl
As it cooked I held my nose
Now the hardest part of all

Is keeping it a secret
From yours truly you know who
Until the time is perfect
And there's nothing left to do

But douse the lights and don
My masterly disguise
I can't wait to see my face
When I shout out Surprise!

Pearl

Pearl was a girl
A pearly girl
But not a girly girl
Not a softly softly
Sssssshhhhhh girl
Not a tiptoe
Through the tulips girl

Pearl was a girl
A pearly girl
But not a girly girl
Not a frills and frippery
Flowery girl
Not a powder puff
Perfume pompom girl

Pearl was a girl
A pearly girl
But not a girly girl
Not a dainty delicate
Dew drop girl
Not a lavender lacy
Look at me me me girl

But a pearl. A pearl of a girl.

Ship in a bottle

My uncle D never sailed the high seas
He builds ships in bottles instead
Using sturdy bamboo and special glue
And a cast for the figurehead

He paints and pencils, traces and stencils
It's the most fantastical thing
Best of all is when he gives me a call
And together we pull the string

Up goes the bowsprit the masts and the booms
As we work at the bottle's neck
The main sail, the stay sail, the sky and the moon
Ahoy! It's all hands on deck!

Hoist up the anchor, a farewell to land
And we're off to sail the high seas
Batten down hatches, adventure's at hand
For the captain and first mate Me!

Sir BB

Sir BB was a knight
Of abundant ability

He fought a silent battle
Against an unseen enemy

He tossed and turned
He wrestled and railed

He fought the itch to run
He fought the yen to wail

He looked past the shadows
To a field of countless sheep

He counted and he counted
And he put himself to sleep

Some Kids

Some kids have a mum and a dad
I've got Aunty Bern who's not half bad
Some kids have computers inside their room
My window shines with stars and moon
Some kids are driven to school and picked up
I get to walk, run, hop, skip and jump
Some kids swim in private swimming pools
I dive in search of the ocean's jewels
Some kids get lessons in ballet and tap
I learn tongue twisters on Aunty Bern's lap
Some kids spend weekends down at the mall
I run my weekend lemonade stall
Some kids have dogs that roll over and beg
My best friend's a chook (a dog can't lay an egg!)
Some kids are named after movie stars
My name was pulled from an old jam jar
Some kids know their way all about town
I know where ants live deep under ground
Some kids have money and mobile phones
I fill my pockets with skipping stones
Some kids have a mum and a dad
I've got Aunty Bern and I'm glad, glad, glad!

Have you seen my lizard

Blue lizards, pink lizards
Stripy, spotty, skink lizards
Lizards lounging on sun-drenched rocks…

But have you seen *my* lizard
The one in football socks?

Smooth lizards, rough lizards
Flat detachable tailed lizards
Lizards with perfect sight…

But have you seen *my* lizard
The one flying the kite?

Frilled lizards, bearded lizards
Shiny, teeny-tiny lizards
Lizards that can swallow cats…

But have you seen *my* lizard
The one in the cowboy hat?

Short lizards, long lizards,
Dust-kicking, lip-licking lizards
Lizards dining on fleas…

But have you seen *my* lizard
The one that looks like me?

If you do see my lizard
Out there on his own
Tell that him I miss him
And won't he please come home.

Home

Lily and Leo and Tully and Fin
Wanted to go where they'd never been
So they packed their bags
And said their goodbyes
Leaving their little house behind

Later whispered Lily
Later-gator! Leo rhymed
H o o r o o sang Tully
And Fin said MINE!

Away skipped the children
Without any cares
Through playgrounds and parks
With trees shaped like bears

What fun whispered Lily
Fun-sun Leo rhymed
H i l a r i o u s sang Tully
And Fin said MINE!

Up over the hill
And into the town
Two sisters two brothers
And the sun going down

It's big whispered Lily
Big-gig Leo rhymed
G i n o r m o u s sang Tully
And Fin said MINE!

They saw the museum
The zoo and the river
But the sun soon went down
And the air made them shiver

I'm cold whispered Lily
Cold-mould Leo rhymed
F r e e z i n g sang Tully
And Fin said MINE!

So back through the town
Up over the hill
They skipped they jogged
They ran from the chill

Through playgrounds and parks
With trees shaped like bears
To the street that they knew
And the house that was theirs

Home whispered Lily
Home-grown Leo rhymed
F a m i l y sang Tully
And they all said MINE

Gotta love that dream

Gotta love that dream.
You know the one I mean?

The one where you get to be
        you.

Not mummy's boy or daddy's girl
or that special little dude,

not big sister little sister
or cousin twice removed,

nobody's pushover
rough and tumble stuff,

not the kid that knows too much
or doesn't know enough.

Gotta love that dream
you know the one I mean?

The one where you get to be
        you

The one where you get to
        be.

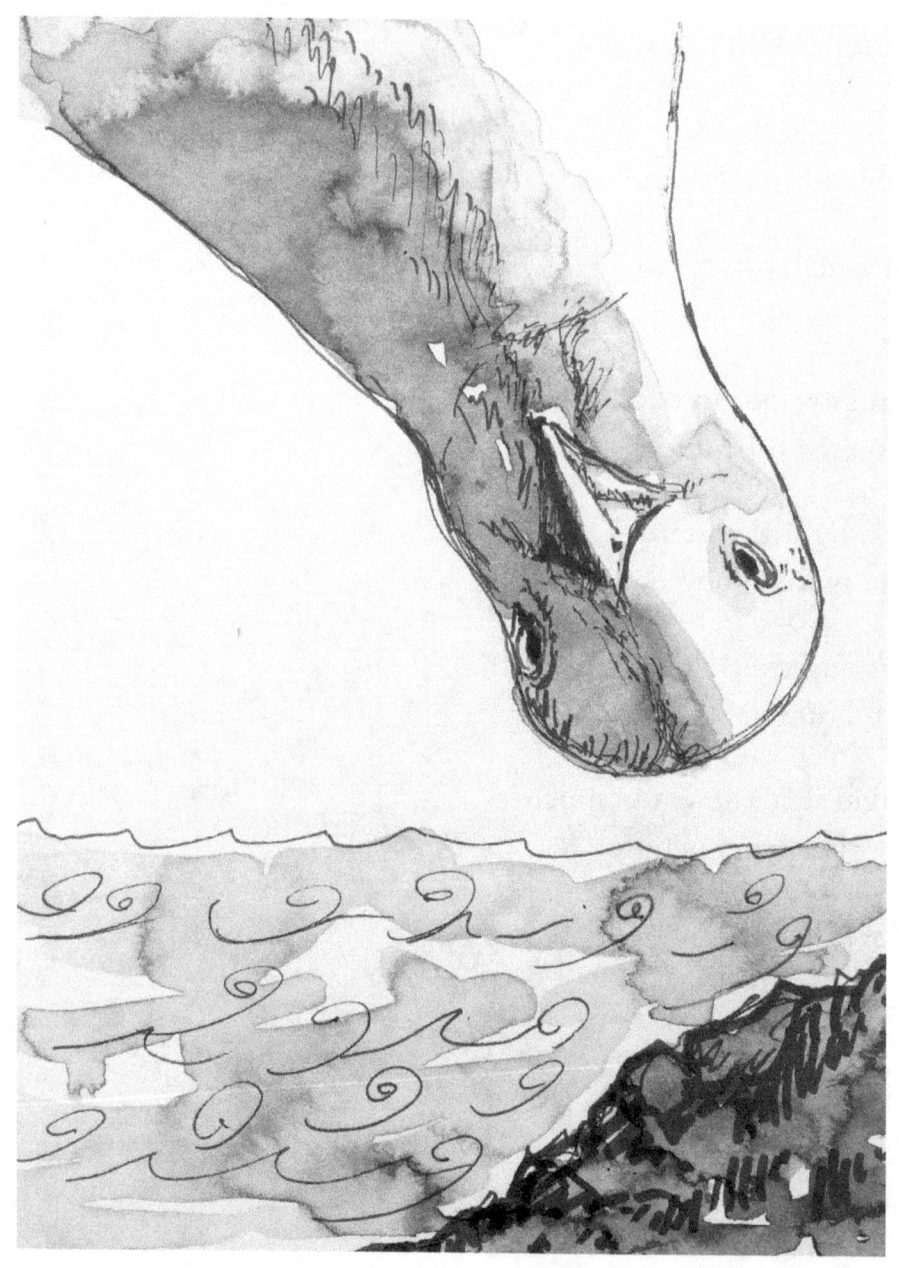

The seagull ~~squawks~~ speaks

Hey you!
You're looking at me like
you've got something to say –
Well OK then
I'm up for a chat,
a chitter, a chatter,
a yabber, a yak,
a tittle-tattle
jibber-jabber,
a yammering yap.
I'm open to suggestion
on topics for discussion.
Let's communicate, confabulate,
wag the chin and chew the fat.
Let's prattle and babble,
let's talk, talk, talk!
But first you've got to learn
how to screech, how to squawk –
so stretch out your neck,
now open your beak…
wait…what's that?
You don't have a beak?
Beg pardon, my mistake
for presuming you could speak!

Animal dreams

If I were a dog
With a tasty bone
I'd dream a deep hole
To bury it down

If I were a cat
That got stuck in trees
I'd dream all trees
Were the same size as me

If I were a cheddar
Cheese-loving mouse
I'd dream yellow bricks
And build me a house

And if I were a
Travelling circus bear
I'd dream fat fish leaping
Through the clean fresh air

Awoooooooooooooo

It's one of those shape-shifty
full moon nights
I'm sick in my bed looking out
when the dogs in the street
begin to howl
Awooooooooooooo

Skipper the Lab from number four
followed by Gypsy the greyhound
then Petal the pug
Bella and Scottie the terrier twins
give it a go to fit in
Awooooooooooooo

It's one of those shape-shifty
full moon nights
Something's growling
in my stomach
now in my chest
now in my throat
some bored and restless thing
ready to let itself out
Awooooooooooooo

www.ingramcontent.com/pod-product-compliance
Lightning Source LLC
Chambersburg PA
CBHW081422080526
44589CB00016B/2634